*A Love Letter to
Texas Women*

A Love
Letter to
Texas
Women

Sarah
Bird

UNIVERSITY OF TEXAS PRESS, AUSTIN

Requests for permission to reproduce material
from this work should be sent to:
Permissions
University of Texas Press
P.O. Box 7819
Austin, TX 78713-7819
http://utpress.utexas.edu/index.php/rp-form

∞ The paper used in this book meets the minimum
requirements of ANSI/NISO Z39.48-1992 (R1997)
(Permanence of Paper).

Library of Congress Cataloging-in-Publication Data
Names: Bird, Sarah, author.
Title: A love letter to Texas women / Sarah Bird.
Description: First edition. Austin : University of Texas Press, 2016.
Identifiers: LCCN 2015038359
ISBN 9781477309490 (cloth : alk. paper)
ISBN 9781477309643 (library e-book)
ISBN 9781477309650 (nonlibrary e-book)
Subjects: LCSH: Women—Texas—Humor. Texas—History—
20th century. Texas—Social life and customs—Humor.
Classification: LCC PS3552.I74 L68 2016

doi:10.7560/309490

"THE YELLOW ROSE OF TEXAS"

You may talk about your Dearest May,
And sing of Rosa Lee,
But the Yellow Rose of Texas
Beats the belles of Tennessee.

TRADITIONAL AMERICAN FOLK SONG

*M*e and the Texas Woman, it was not love at first sight. In fact, my match with her was a bit of an arranged marriage. One with a rocky start, potholed by cultural misunderstandings and distrust. It took decades of observation to fully appreciate the Yellow Rose in all her glories. All her contradictions. All her glorious contradictions.

Was she Southern? All belles and balls? Or was she Western? Ready to rope and ride and shoot the head off a rattler? You already know the answer. You know, that like sulfur, charcoal, and bat guano, the ingredients don't really pop until they're mixed up together into gunpowder. The Texas Woman is a hybrid with all the vig-

or that comes from the perfect pairing of the best of two species. She is Southern but with the Western grit handed down by her foremothers, who could give birth during a Comanche attack, help out when it came time to turn the bulls into steers, and still end up producing more Miss USAs than any other state in the union.

Whichever end of the geographical spectrum you want to come at her from, there is something undeniably special about the Texas Woman. Perhaps you doubt this statement and question her alleged "specialness." Perhaps, at this very moment, you are considering the Texas Women of your acquaintance—your mother, your sisters, your sorority sisters, your suitemates at SMU, the moms you carpool with, your partners at the firm, the gals in your book-slash-white-wine-swilling club. You might even be reflecting upon the worthiness of your own dainty self. Possibly you have concluded that your birth and subsequent flowering in the Lone Star State have not distinguished you in any way beyond an unnatural fondness for Dr Pepper and queso.

Well, guess what? It doesn't matter whether or not you believe you are special, because the rest of the world does. Travel around the globe and mention to, oh, say, a Frenchman that you are from any other state in the country, Iowa, for example, and you won't get a rhapsodic ode to corn or really much beyond a Gallic shrug. But reveal that you hail from *Tex-ASS*, *et mon dieu*. Responses will range from *oooh-la-la*—possibly accompanied by a volley of finger pistol shots fired into the air with sound effects translated—*Pan! Pan! Pan!*—to questions about the size of your vast ranch, the horses you surely ride, and, inevitably, George W. Bush, the Iraq War, and your personal responsibility for both of them.

The Beach Boys might have wished they all could be California girls, but, really, can't that dream be attained with some highlights and a few hours in a tanning booth? As a Texas Woman, on the other hand, you come with your very own set of hand-tooled baggage. You arrive with an indelible brand, an identity, a belief that there is something special about you and all the ladies of the Lone Star State that defines a girl in a way that birth in any other state doesn't begin to approach. This uniqueness isn't always of the special "good" variety. But it's definitely of the special "different" category. And there are some fine reasons for this belief. Deep historical and cultural reasons. Reasons that I didn't have the first clue about when fate and good love gone bad deposited me here in the great state of.

I was the most reluctant of Texas transplants. It was 1973, and I was a newly minted graduate of the University of New Mexico as well as a board-certified hippie when my college sweetheart announced that he was moving to Texas to take some courses. I was horrified. Texas? At that historical moment, Texas represented everything my patchouli-scented pals and I detested. I never would have moved here except for my utter certainty that life would not have been worth living without the aforementioned Smooch Nugget.

When I revealed to my friends that I was moving to Texas, they too went into shock. Upon recovery, they threw a farewell party and presented me with what they considered to be the essentials for my new life as a Texas Woman: three cans of Aqua Net hairspray; a pair of red plastic Kmart cowgirl boots; a toy six-shooter; and a Gideon's Bible, recently purloined on my behalf. What would my friends have given me if I'd been moving to Wisconsin? A tub of cheese curds?

Branding? The Texas Woman put a lock on that concept decades before anyone else had even heard of it.

Upon arriving in Austin, the first place my boyfriend took me to visit was, as is required by law, the UT Tower, where Charles Whitman shot fourteen innocents. Next he whisked me away to the Stallion Restaurant and insisted that I order one of their famous ninety-nine-cent chicken-fried steaks. Alongside a glass of iced tea, strangely presweetened and delivered in a tankard the size of a wastebasket, I was served the largest piece of meat I had ever seen not roaming a feed lot. I was certain that, between the dangers of mass murderers and consuming fried meat patties the size of hubcaps, my darling would recognize Texas for the existential threat it was and we would decamp for the Land of Enchantment before you could say "cardiac arrest."

Alas, an entirely different form of heartache awaited me. A stranger in a strange land, I was further marked as an outsider by my lack of a car in a world built upon petrochemicals. As I pedaled the unfamiliar streets in search of a job, I was everywhere assailed by the screech of grackles and by Texans' mauling of the English language. What was this "all" they pumped from the ground? And who might "Bob" with the last name of "War" be? And where was "Biler" University located? Spanish fared even worse. Was "Gwadaloop" a guacamole-flavored breakfast cereal as opposed to Our Lady of?

Frankly, I could have rolled with a few linguistic eccentricities except for one small problem back at the love nest: Lord Yum Yum was hardly ever home. Of course, I suspected some Texas floozy of having lured my beloved into her clutches. I visualized a heavily highlighted Farrah Fawcettesque temptress flashing a smile (clearly bleached) and batting her eyelashes (obviously fake) at Cuddle Cakes. I imagined her drenching my darling in honeyed diphthongs whispered through lips glossed like she'd survived an oil spill. Coming from counterculture Albuquerque, where any woman caught wearing more makeup than a swipe of ChapStick was considered a traitor to the feminist cause, I knew that my innocent New Mexico boy had no native resistance to the cosmetic arts that had reached such a high state of perfection in Texas. He would be a sucker for the Texas Woman's perfectly plucked brow, her well-applied base coat, and her masterfully contoured and blushed cheekbones.

Who was I kidding? He'd be a goner with his first glimpse of a shaved leg. Texas Women had skills we rawboned New Mexico gals couldn't even begin to compete with.

So it was with great trepidation that I confronted him with my suspicions. Yes, he admitted, he had fallen for another. But it wasn't a Texas Woman. It was L. Ron Hubbard. What I had assumed were graduate school classes turned out to be Scientology courses.

Because I so desperately wanted the relationship to work, I submitted to an introductory course to try to understand this strange obsession. The class was like a combination of old-school assertiveness training and a five-year-old's birthday party. We played Simon Says. We played it the way it would have been played in the Prussian army. We had staring contests of eye-parching duration. The first one to blink didn't just lose; they lost in a cosmically significant way.

Though I wanted to believe more than any heretic stretched out on the rack ever wanted to believe, my doubts only increased. So I did what I'd done for every other problem, obstacle, or mystery I'd ever faced in my pre-Internet life: I went to the library to research. After a bit of digging into Lord Xenu and a few of Scientology's more flamboyant intergalactic beliefs, I shared the opinion with my boyfriend that his new club was a sci-fi pyramid scheme.

Overnight, a Gaza Strip of irreconcilable differences sprang up between us and we became an interfaith couple. A head-spinningly short time later, we were dividing up the record albums. He left Joni Mitchell and Linda Ronstadt behind so that I'd have lots of music to weep to. Then he hit the road for LA and a new life working at Scientology's Celebrity Centre.

I'm certain I would have slunk back to New Mexico had I not received a fellowship to study journalism at the University of Texas and found new lodgings two blocks from campus at Seneca House Co-op for Graduate Women. Seneca House was just like a UT sorority, if there were ever a sorority where no woman plucked her eyebrows or used deodorant; where the sisters stayed up all night arguing about what the French deconstructionists were *really* trying to say; and where everyone was eating quinoa at a time when the only other humans consuming that hearty grain were Quechua Indians. Did I think all Lone Starlets glopped on the makeup? The residents of Seneca House,

*The former Varsity House becomes Seneca House
as my fellow residents hang the new sign.*

faces scrubbed cleaner than any Amish girl's, proved how wrong I was. Still, even in her ungilded state, I was not yet able to open my heart to the Yellow Rose.

No, that awakening occurred at the Lyndon Baines Johnson Presidential Library, where the great State of Texas and my skill at resumé puffery had delivered unto me a job as a temporary archivist. There, while cataloguing photos of LBJ hiking up his shirt to display his scar from gallbladder surgery or hoisting his beagles, Him and Her, up by their long, floppy ears, then later filing the subsequent letters of protest from animal lovers around the country—"Deer Mr. President. Stop it! You are the most meanest president I no. Stephanie Hudgins. Third Grade."—I came to know and love Lady Bird Johnson. Because, really, say what you or Robert Caro might about LBJ, who doesn't love Lady Bird?

Has there ever been a finer paragon of Texas Womanhood than our country's thirty-sixth First Lady, Claudia Alta Taylor Johnson? Born in Karnack, Texas, deep in the Piney Woods, she had the Southern belle graciousness to understand that we all need a bit of beauty in our lives, whether it be highways lined with wildflowers where only billboards and junkyards had blossomed before or inner-city DC parks transformed into oases of dogwood trees and azaleas. The Highway Beautification Act of 1965 is so much Claudia Alta's baby that it was nicknamed Lady Bird's Bill.

But this East Texas lass, who lost her mother at the age of five, also had plenty of pioneer woman, Wagons Ho! grit stiffening her spine. And though, in keeping with the mores of the times, she always presented herself as a modest housewife, it was Lady Bird who, using a small inheritance, financed LBJ's first congressional run, and later purchased the radio and TV stations that would insure the family's future financial security. Never was the Texas Woman gumption that allowed a shy, motherless child to become a tireless campaigner on behalf of both Kennedy's election and the Civil Rights Act more evident than it was when she stood resolutely by her man through the dark hours after the assassination of John F. Kennedy and, later, when the Vietnam War tore apart the country and her husband's legacy.

Though I doubt that Lady Bird oversaw this one, I catalogued photos from another beautification project that took place during LBJ's presidency. I speak of the makeover that Lady Bird's daughter, the magnolia-skinned Lynda Bird, underwent for her "dream date" with the mahogany-tanned George Hamilton. *Life* magazine detailed every step of a process that involved plucking away Lynda's lovely widow's-peak hairline, applying Big Bird eyelashes to her luminous eyes, and spackling her ivory skin into geisha paleness. I couldn't have said what my heroine Lady Bird made of that transformation; I did, however, discern a loving maternal hand behind another surprise discovery.

While most of the large brown boxes I hauled down for cataloguing were heavy as manhole covers, filled as they were with photos and reams of paper, one day I yanked a box down that seemed empty. It wasn't. Inside the large brown box were dozens and dozens of small, heart-shaped boxes covered in white satin and adorned with red, curlicue script. Within each white box a nickel-sized packet wrapped in red foil nestled upon a doily. Unable to resist, I opened one of the packets, and found a leathery brown puck. Divining that the puck had once been edible, I popped it into my mouth and bit down. Over the years, the morsel had become so thoroughly metallized that it set up an electrical charge between my back molars as if I had chomped down directly on the red foil.

Another *Life* article, this one devoted to Lynda Bird's White House wedding to her gallant Marine captain Chuck Robb, revealed the secret of the mystery puck: it was a sliver of the groom's fruitcake. I clung to the belief that Lady Bird had orchestrated these favors so that guests could take home a souvenir of the historic White House ceremony. And, since it *was* fruitcake, they could regift it in perpetuity.

Though every article about or photo of Lady Bird that I ever catalogued conveyed nothing but benevolence, I didn't experience this quality myself until the end of my summer job at the LBJ Library. That was when I and all the other temps were gathered up and escorted to the tenth floor. After spending three months in the windowless gloom of the fifth floor, where I'd labored all alone with no company but the snores of my fellow temp, a musician who spent his days resting up for that evening's gig, this was like ascending to heaven. A reception with punch and store-bought cookies was set up in the Presidential Suite. For the first time, all of us Mole People gazed out of the solid bank of windows that crown the library and beheld the finest view of Austin imaginable. A flock of grackles winged past at eye level. The forty acres of the university lay at our feet, pretty as a Tyrolean village.

Seneca House's whole-grain, sprouts, and spelt menu left me perpetually starved for what had previously been my best friend: sugar. As I was stuffing in the chocolate thumbprint and molasses lace cookies, the door opened, and men in black suits speaking into their cuffs ushered Lady Bird in. What they say about celebrity encounters is true: people you know from magazines and television always seem smaller in person. Lady Bird, delicate and demure in a sunshine-yellow A-line dress, appeared as birdlike as her nickname, a bright chick in the escort of ravens.

She welcomed us lowly temps as if we were all friends of her daughters who'd been invited over for a slumber party. I will never forget the moment when she pressed my chocolate-smudged hand between both of hers, tilted her head to the side, smiled, looked me in the eye, and, in her carefully enunciated drawl, thanked me for my service. Decades later Jan Jarboe Russell, legendary Texas journalist and author of *Lady Bird: A Biography of Mrs. Johnson*, would tell me, "When anyone was in the presence of Lady Bird, it was impossible not to feel that she carried within her a love of invisible beauty. She carried a kind of reverence that anyone could sense." That reverence came across as a kindness so essential that it compelled her to take time from her packed schedule to meet with an anonymous group of minimum-wagers. An instant later, Lady Bird slid her hand from mine, the ravens closed in, and she was gone.

School began at the same time that a tropical monsoon—or so it seemed to this desert transplant—deluged Austin. Still heartbroken, the skies and I wept ceaselessly. My toothbrush, towel, and pillowcase were never dry. A velvety green fuzz of mildew blossomed on my shoes. When the rains finally stopped, the steamy city turned into a sickroom with a vaporizer on overdrive. My hair, straight as uncooked spaghetti in New Mexico, went Medusa in the humidity. Meanwhile, Seneca House had received a bright new crop of residents. None of them brighter than the girl from Houston who bounced in one exceedingly swampy day and asked in a voice as perky as that of any Kilgore Rangerette, "Don't all y'all just love Austin? It's so dry-y-y-y-y-y here!"

The amount of information contained in that bewildering pronouncement was as dense as antimatter. I learned so much from her statement. I learned that the plural of "y'all" is "all y'all." I learned that dry contains five syllables. And I learned that I must never set foot in Houston until I'd grown gills. While my new housemate beamed away, waiting for my response, a memory surfaced: this was not my first time at this particular rodeo. I had encountered the Texas Woman's relentless friendliness before, as the child of an Air Force officer stationed in San Antonio.

That meeting hadn't fully registered because the first Texas Woman I ever met had still been in her larval stage, the Texas Girl. Besides, having grown up in an Air Force family, I found the entire concept of state identity inconceivable. In the military, especially on the overseas bases where I'd spent so many years of my childhood, a state is nothing more than one of fifty fingers ready to be balled up into a fist and used to smite the enemies of these United States. The thumb doesn't say, "I'm a proud Thumbian!" The little finger isn't forever reminding all the other digits, "I hail from the great state of Pinkiana!" No, you're a hand. Period. End of story. End of state identity.

We were transferred to Brooks Air Force Base in far south San Antonio right before I started seventh grade. My parents did what all good Catholic parents were advised to do at the time: send your children to parochial school or, oh, burn in hell for all eternity. So, off I went to Holy Name Catholic School, shell-shocked from having moved far more often than was healthy for a child of my catatonically shy, temperamentally tense nature. I didn't actually mind the moves; it was the new schools that were torture. There had been five in fifth grade. For me, new schools were a prison situation. The best I ever hoped for was to be ignored. To blend in and do my time without getting punked or shanked.

Which is why, when a gang of Texas Girls approached me on the playground,

I reacted with the suspicious prickliness of Easterners and other stiff-necked Yankee types. I figured they'd either steal my lunch money or stab me with the very nifty clip-on tie that, along with a cunning navy blue beanie, made our Catholic schoolgirl uniforms the dazzling fashion statements that they were. Once I surrendered, accepting the stunning reality that these strangers wanted nothing more than to be friends, I found myself in a world where no one was excluded. Where everyone had a place. Where everyone was invited. Whether it was to a record party in someone's garage or a full-blown *quinceañera*. I don't know if I should thank Holy Mother Church for this uncommon warmth or credit the influence of *las mexicanas* for creating a Mean Girl–free world where, for the first time ever, I had friends. With no evidence beyond my own experience to back this up, I'm going to give props to the humanizing effect of Latina culture. Thanks to *mis amigas*, I spent the happiest years of my childhood in San Antonio. Both of them.

And that is what I remembered as I confronted this mature version of the Texas Girl, waiting for me to comment on her observation about the humidity. "I guess it's all relative," I muttered, and thus began a friendship that, like those with my bow-tied and beanied buddies, has endured to this day. I didn't know it at the time, but my exorbitantly outgoing new housemate was displaying a skill characteristic of the Yellow Rose, "neighboring."

I would not hear this enchanting term or understand the concept until one year later, when I did my graduate thesis at a beauty shop. By then I had lateraled over from journalism to photojournalism. A

Checking out my first photojournalism
assignment shot with a Polaroid.

camera was my passport out of shyness. It arrived stamped with visas for any place I wanted to explore. With a Nikon in front of my face, I became invisible, free to stalk and observe any subject I chose. And the subject I chose most often was the Texas Woman. I was especially partial to documenting her grooming behaviors, and took to lurking around parlors, shoppes, even a beauty college. But my hands-down favorite was a charmingly dowdy place, the Hyde Park Beauty Salon.

The Hyde Park was a vintage holdover from the days of permanent waves and towering beehive hairdos. Sadly, it was long ago gobbled up by Austin's metastasizing hipsterism. (I believe it was replaced by a craft beer joint that also sells fixed-gear bikes, vinyl records, feed for urban chickens, and mustache wax.) In its day, however, the salon was a secret clubhouse for neighborhood women, where they caught up on all the gossip and hid out for a few hours from housework, kids, and the menfolk.

A bell tinkled when you opened the door and then the Hyde Park's signature scent hit you. The shop smelled of the eye-stinging ammonia in hair dye, the ozone-busting aerosols in hair spray, burnt coffee, and the brownies, cookies, or salads that the patrons inevitably brought in to share. The ladies had been coming since before World War II, when they were all young mothers and the shop was brand-new. They came once a week for a wash and set, then cocooned their hair in toilet paper at night to preserve those lacquered coiffures. Mostly, though, they came to be with their friends, the other women in the Hyde Park neighborhood who had seen them through childbearing and raising, drinking husbands, cheating

Sharing a joke and getting ready for a set at the Hyde Park Beauty Salon

Decades of friendship went into every coif
at the Hyde Park Beauty Salon

husbands, divorce, remarriage, retirement, and death.

In a grand old tradition—one observed by former Texas governor Jim Hogg when he gave his daughter the supremely character-building name of Ima Hogg (reports that there was a sister christened "Ura" are apocryphal)—these Texas ladies of a certain age had magnificently flamboyant names: Eddie Faye, Peninah, Waynette, Permelia Lynn, Dicy.

It was from them that I learned what all Southern gals know: anything can be a salad. Unless specifically classed as a "green" salad, it need not, in fact probably would not, contain a single vegetable. One of the patrons of the salon was famous for her Goop Salad. The precise recipe eludes me at the moment, but I am unable to forget these key ingredients: Whip 'n' Chill, green olives, Hellmann's—

none of your Yankee Miracle Whip, thank you very much—and lime Jello. That was a very "green" salad, indeed.

As with my Holy Name buddies, everyone was welcome at the Hyde Park Beauty Salon. Even the schizophrenics who wandered in from the Austin State Hospital across the street. The sweet ladies of the Hyde Park would listen and nod sympathetically as a visitor shared secret messages she'd received from the angel Gabriel or revealed how she had acquired a patent on the concept of time. This last revelation was accompanied by urgent taps on the listener's wristwatch and warnings to the wearer to pay up. Every time she checked her watch, royalties were owed.

Whatever a patron's mental state when she walked in, the gentlewomen of Hyde Park had a secret that invariably made her feel welcome and raised her spirits as high as their voluminous coiffures. And that secret was "neighboring."

At the salon I heard stories about how a woman used to "neighbor" with someone and how a patron was "neighboring up" with a newcomer. Judgments were passed about those who failed to "neighbor." This bone-deep instinct to be friendly to anyone who might cross one's path was the quality I came to admire most in Texas Women. Though I only heard the term a few times after my days at Hyde Park were over, I've never forgotten what I learned about the origins of this most essential of elements in the Yellow Rose genome.

Many of the women's families had moved into town when ranches and farms were lost to drought, depression, or disaster, both natural and man-made. These rural transplants brought with them the wisdom passed down to each Texas Woman by her pioneering foremothers: that her survival, and the survival of her children, might easily depend upon the strangers whom Divine Providence had selected to be her neighbors. She knew that if she didn't befriend those who lived nearby, she would have no one to turn to if her husband fell ill, or the barn burned, or the crops failed, or Indians attacked. Perhaps even more deeply bred into the Texas Woman was her ancestresses' hunger for female companionship. The friendliness that Yankees such as myself found so suspicious was the legacy handed down by women so starved for the company of another female that they had risked their lives to ride or walk the long, dangerous miles to the nearest neighbor woman's house.

Like the camera, the Texas Woman friendliness that the ladies of Hyde Park modeled for me was a passport out of shyness. It opened up an entire tonal range of sociability that, like dog whistles and football commentary, had never been audible to me in the past. In comparison to their effusive overtures, my own previous attempts at friendliness now seemed like the borderline hostile mumblings of a phobic hermit. As in the movie *Spinal Tap*, Texas Women turned my amp up to eleven. I learned that it was almost impossible to overdo expressions of goodwill and kind intentions, and I started broadcasting in a way that, for the first time—thanks to Texas Woman amplification—came across as actual approachability.

I am deeply indebted to Lone Starlets for another essential trait: they teach their men to dance. Long before *Urban Cowboy* made boot-scooting a national phenomenon, Texas was the dancingest state in the union. For this, we must thank

With a new friend at a Native American rodeo.

the intrepid immigrants to our young republic. So, *danke*, dancing *damen*, for bringing your polkas and *schottisches* from Germany. And gracious *gracias* to all you beautiful señoritas, who helped twirl us into your irresistibly danceable *música norteña*. But my biggest thanks have to go to you *ženy* of Czech descent. Without you, I would never have met my husband. Here's the story.

Even after graduate school, I continued my photographic explorations of Texas in all its florid extravagance. No phenomenon fascinated me more than what I came to call "mutant rodeos." These were the hybrids dreamed up by communities outside the mainstream professional rodeo circuit. Fueled by the delusional dream that I might one day publish a photo-essay on my precious weirdo rodeos, I traveled all over the state interviewing and photographing the people who roped and rode in rodeos for kids, girls, Native Americans, police, and prisoners.

I burned out the engine of my spiffy 1973 Vega hatchback visiting *charreadas*, old-timers' rodeos, and gay rodeos from the tip of the Panhandle down to the pointed toe of the Valley. The hands-down most fun events were African American rodeos, held when communities in El Campo, Plum, and Egypt hosted freewheeling reunions that featured picnics, barbecues, and dances to celebrate special events such as Juneteenth. I even heard about a nudist rodeo. Held in California, of course. But I never got close enough to that one to learn the true meaning of bareback riding. To say nothing of raw hide.

One of the first rodeos I ever shot took place during the annual Texas Cowboy Reunion in Stamford. At a dance one

Enjoying a pickle at a Juneteenth rodeo.

evening, I sat on the sidelines marveling at the hydraulic smoothness with which the men led and the women followed one another around a dance floor set up beneath a large, open canopy that gleamed beneath strings of twinkle lights. With all the couples in hats, boots, and snap-button shirts, it was a scene from an old Western. One about ladies bringing civilization to the frontier.

I was startled out of my reverie when one of the rodeo-ers time-traveled out of his dimension long enough to enter mine. With his handlebar mustache, battered Stetson, worn-out boots with the tops accordioning down around the jeans he'd tucked into them, and actual working spurs that jingle-jangled when he walked, he could have stepped off of an old tintype. Though all the alleged cowdudes that night were togged out in their best Marlboro Man gear, most of them were far more likely to be mobile home salesmen or PE teachers than bonafide buckaroos. But here before me was the real deal, a true ride-the-range, working cowboy capable of dosing a steer for screwworm or pulling a breech-birth calf. And he had the teeth, mottled by well water like caramel creams, to prove it. He swept off his hat, displaying Neopolitan stripes of chocolate tan, strawberry sunburn, and a glaring white vanilla forehead, and asked, "Care to dance?"

I told him I didn't know how. At least not at the synchronized swimming–level of dance going on out on the floor.

He acted as if I'd just revealed an inability to breathe. "You can't two-step?"

"Nope, sorry."

"Can you walk?"

I assured him that I was fully ambulatory.

"Then, darlin', you can two-step."

"Darlin'." Texas Women, do you know how lucky you are? In no other state in the union had I ever been addressed as "darlin'."

As for the two-step? It turned out to be just as simple as advertised. As we shuffled around the floor—quick, quick, slow—my new cowpal explained that he came from a Czech ranching family and that every Saturday night, his mama and five sisters "cleart the furniture out the house" and he danced with them all. "We were Catholic," he explained. "Them Babtists, though, they was a whole other deal. Wouldn't even have sex standing up case someone thought they was dancin'." I laughed at the old joke and told him that his sisters and his mama were excellent teachers. At the break he offered me a stick of Juicy Fruit. When I accepted, he asked if I'd like him to "skin" it for me.

I would. He unwrapped the gum and handed it over.

Sometime after the New York publishing world informed me that they'd be delighted to print a book of my offbeat rodeo photos, provided my name was either Annie Leibovitz or Mary Ellen Mark, I found a much more personal reason to be grateful for the Texas Woman's dance imperative when I attended a music festival that used to be held annually on the banks of Austin's Lady Bird Lake. Okay, "festival" might be stretching it a bit. "Big outdoor drunk with unruly mobs occasionally shuffling around to music as an excuse to touch strangers" would probably be a better way to describe Aqua Fest. In any event, many grain-based beverages had been consumed by the time I spotted an especially fetching lad. The *ur*-two-step "San Antonio Rose" was playing and, courage fortified and lessons from Mama intact, I asked him to dance.

He accepted, but, by the time we made it onto the floor, the band was rolling out the barrels and striking up a rollicking Dusseldorf-by-way-of-New Braunfels polka. The fine-looking stranger and I galloped through several intensely cardiovascular oompah numbers until a break for more malted beverages was required. Our moves were considerably smoother when we waltzed together at our wedding four years later. (We'd been married secretly for three of those years. But that is a story of true love and major medical deductibles best saved for another time.)

Finding me a husband would have been miracle enough to win the Texas Woman a permanent place in my heart, but there was more. She also paved the way for my career.

My first novel, *Alamo House*, drew heavily upon my days at Seneca House and my amazement at the multitudinous stupefactions I'd encountered in the Lone Star State. In this book, I savagely satirized the UT Longhorns and their dangerously delusional obsession with football. I mercilessly mocked the crunchy granola, counterculture pretensions of the co-opers. I laceratingly lampooned the grandiosity of the LBJ Library. But I saved my most acidic vitriol for the frat boys across the street from Seneca House, who had tortured us with greetings of "Hey, lesbo-dyke-whores!" and endless, eardrum-bursting, GPA-shattering parties. In my mind, I gutted them, every one. I was sure that the instant my screed was published, I would be run out of town on a rail.

Instead, to my astonishment, every single one of the camps that I was certain would be pressing legal action embraced the novel. The head of the real fraternity on which I had based my Sigma Upsilon Kappas, the Sucks, called to say they were putting copies in every chapter in the country as a cautionary tale. A UT task force asked for advice about reforms to the Greek system. Former sorority sisters invited me to speak at their book clubs. I still receive letters from old coopers thanking me for capturing their world with such accuracy and affection. And, although the LBJ Library initially declared a *fatwa* upon me, a director appointed many years after the feelings hurt by my first novel had been salved even arranged for me and a reporter from the *Austin American-Statesman* to revisit those heart-shaped boxes; *Alamo House* readers had made so many inquiries that a special wedding cake tour had been made available.

The most unexpected supporter of my warts-and-all portrayal of campus life, though, was an unpretentious West Texas girl who, nurtured by an abiding love of books, grew up on—Dickensian clue ahead!—Humble Avenue in Midland, and went on to become the second First Lady that Texas has sent to the White House. Though Laura Bush and I were in graduate school at UT at the same time and, by all accounts, enjoyed many of the same delights in a city where the counterculture *was* the culture, I was still flabbergasted when she selected me to be one of the readers at a celebration of her husband's 1995 gubernatorial victory. Because the event was held on the UT campus and because it took place on MLK Day and because I had been a very vocal backer of Bush's opponent, Ann Richards, I felt an obligation to wave the liberal banner. I was certain that the flaming defense of the progressive agenda I delivered that day would extinguish Laura Bush's goodwill and put a stop to her nonsectarian invitations forever. Instead, a week later her office got in touch to request a copy of my reading: an aunt of Mrs. Bush's had enjoyed it.

During Bush's second term as governor, I was included in a gathering for Texas artists held at the mansion. I wore a navy blue pantsuit that made me look like I was in the Secret Service. I thought that explained why Governor Bush sidled up to me and, as irresistible as the funniest, naughtiest kid in class, began kidding around. Assuming he had no idea who I was, I was astonished when he joked, "So you're the one making my wife laugh in bed at night." My love for the man's wife was sealed that day.

As First Lady of Texas, Laura Bush, holder of a master's degree in library science, proved herself to be a truly genuine and truly bipartisan lover of both books and their authors. She threw herself wholeheartedly into organizing Texas's first book festival and ensuring that the invited writers came from both ends of the political spectrum and many places in between. In 2000 the festival occurred during one of the most tumultuous moments in our country's history: those fraught days when the results of the Gore v. Bush election hung in the balance. Though the whole country was losing its mind, Laura proceeded calmly with festival business, welcoming/neighboring up with visiting authors, monitoring the book sales that help support libraries around the country, and attending sessions whenever she could. Stephen Harrigan, one of her chosen speakers, observed at that year's opening gala that, for the duration of Laura's festival, "we aren't a democracy of the left or a democracy of the right; we are a democracy of books."

Though I went on to march in many protests against Laura Bush's husband, just as I'd marched in many protests against Lady Bird Johnson's husband, I admired both first ladies for their nuanced brand of Texas Woman pioneer grit. They both embraced, for the entirety of their careers, the complexities of marriages that are beyond the comprehension of anyone who hasn't been required to be publicly worshipful of her husband for years on end. Both of these resilient Roses remained steadfastly loyal to complicated, driven, and bedeviled men and to unions that subjected them to an inhuman degree of scrutiny. And they each did so with an undeniable Southern graciousness.

Laura Bush's surprising response to my first novel, mirrored throughout the state, taught me a simple truth: Texas leads the country in allowing women to be funny. As if there were ever any other possibility. Coming from foremothers who faced down twisters, prairie fires, and blue northers that turned cattle into ice sculptures; who lost children to diphtheria, cholera, scarlet fever, and malaria; and who educated generations of backwoods lunkheads in one-room schoolhouses, Lone Star ladies have deep wells of pioneer stoicism to draw upon. According to the cowgirl code, complaining isn't cool, and high marks are given to those who can laugh in the face of hardship and turn tough times into jokes. The undisputed queens of this art are, of course, the irreplaceable Molly Ivins and Ann Richards.

If the Texas Woman ever had an ambassador, Molly was it. Not only did she spread the Texas Woman brand like no one before or since, she so thoroughly transformed herself into its living embodiment that she was sometimes derided as a "professional Texan" and taken to task for transforming her River Oaks/Smith College/Columbia University accent into the hickest of hick drawls. Those who mocked her for performing Texas Woman drag missed the point. How else was a six-foot-tall redhead of Valkyrian proportions, who burned with idealism yet grew up in a world of girdles and white gloves—a world where women were rewarded for being cute and being quiet—ever supposed to make herself heard?

How, one might ask those critics, do they think the right-wingers and Jesus-mongers would have received a Yankee-sounding, *female* intellectual who insisted on dragging them to the High Holy Church of Progressive Ideals? Probably with a resounding silence, since they would never have been able to receive on the pointy-headed lady egghead frequency. Which is why, on the taped version of her best-seller *You Got to Dance with Them What Brung You*, when Molly declares her undying allegiance to all that is right and Leftie, she translates it into pure Redneckese, drawling, "There's nuthin' you kin do 'bout bein' barn liberal."

(Quick side note to those who also sneer about Molly's love of fermented bevs. Yeah, she drank. It was the price of admission. If you needed inside info about the Lege, you got it from men. At bars. And you paid for it with your liver.)

I first learned exactly how powerful Molly was in spreading the Texas Woman brand in the fall of 1991, when I was touring with the book that finally came out of my rodeo research, my fourth novel, *Virgin of the Rodeo*. Molly Ivins had just published her breakout book, *Molly Ivins Can't Say That, Can She?*, and I had the misfortune of visiting cities right after her. I say misfortune because the one person you never, ever wanted to follow was Molly Ivins. No one could follow her. Certainly not me. In empty bookstore after empty bookstore from Seattle to Manhattan, I was reminded of just how far short I fell of her gold standard of Texas Womanhood. Again and again I was told that I "should have been here last week when Molly was here." It was always "Molly," and her devotees always spoke of her as if she were the best friend they didn't get to see often enough, but whose visit was the highlight of the year.

When I finally met her, Molly was as unfailingly kind and generous to me as she was to every writer who ever crossed her freakishly noncompetitive path. I, on the other hand, was too much of a starstruck, tongue-tied fangirl for us to ever become actual friends. How I regret my dopiness.

Not too long ago, when NPR's Moth Radio Hour taped a show at the Paramount Theater in Austin, I was selected to be the hometown representative. I joined a few of the show's old favorites from around the country in trying to live up to the program's goal of real stories, told live, without notes. Emcees of the Moth have a tradition of asking their storytellers a question by way of introduction. My question was, "What person, alive or dead, would you most like to meet? And why?" Thinking only about how I would give anything to have a do-over meeting with Molly, one where I wouldn't be an awestruck goofball, I blurted out, "Molly Ivins." As to the why, I said, "Because she was the only hero I've ever had." When I concluded with,

"Oh, Molly, I miss her still."

"Oh, Molly, I miss her still," the sold-out crowd of 1,200 brought the house down, whooping and applauding and generally making the kind of ruckus that only rock stars and politicos with bought crowds can raise.

One politician who never needed to buy love was Ann Richards, the inimitable Lone Star lady who pointed out to the country that Bush the Elder was born with a silver foot in his mouth and that Ginger Rogers did everything that Fred Astaire did; she just did it backwards and in high heels. While Molly might have been the Texas Woman brand ambassador, Ann was her icon. That trademark tornado of white hair whirling above those electric blue eyes and that gloriously uncorrected set of Shar Pei neck wrinkles were as unforgettable as they were unmistakably Ann.

Only now, as Hillary Clinton is poised

to become the first woman with a serious shot at the presidency, can we truly assess Ann's significance. As Jan Reid, the impeccable journalist and author of *Let the People In: The Life and Times of Ann Richards*, reminds us, "Ann was the first ardent feminist elected to major office in this country. Hillary Clinton considered Ann her mentor when she was First Lady and then the Senator from New York. After Ann, politics and government in Texas could never go back to the old white-boys' club it had been since the end of Reconstruction. A lot of the cracks in the glass ceiling that we hear so much about were put there by Ann."

In an astonishing abundance of riches, our state gave us not one but two women who not only spoke truth to power but who delivered it in stand-up-ready punch lines that won more hearts and minds than LBJ ever dreamed of. Ann and Molly. Whether you agreed or dis-agreed with them, you couldn't deny that there was a quality of fearlessness about both that was pure Texas Woman.

Fearless. There's a label that is tossed around awfully freely these days. Essay-ists are called fearless for writing about how motherhood bores them. Female comics are lauded for their bravery in stating that they think they're pretty even if they're overweight. Memoirists get courage cred for writing about their amped-up sexuality and battles with bu-limia. Though it certainly does take nerve to invite the world into the messiness of one's inner life, I wonder if it might not be time to recalibrate what constitutes fearlessness.

Maybe, before awarding anyone the title "fearless," we ought to consider the kind of bravery that it took for Ann, a di-vorceé and survivor of a very public battle with alcoholism, to run for and win the governorship of a state that was a bastion of good-ole-boy cronyism. Demonstrations of sheer physical courage should probably also be required for admission into the ranks of the fearless. Physical courage of the sort demonstrated by Molly Ivins, a single woman living alone, who, in the face of death threats, never stopped naming names and indicting the powerful as she wrote about social injustice, institutionalized racism, political chicanery, the blistering stupidity of the Texas "Lege," and the tragic inadequacy of the Bush she christened Shrub.

We might also want to consider subject matter before we hand out the Purple Hearts. While laughs are good wherever you can get them, whether the joke is your boyfriend's porn addiction or your intense feelings about selfie sticks, let's consider Molly's amazing achievement of commenting on the vital issues of the day, most of them complete with buttons so hot that even today few dare touch them. Then let's add being so funny for so long while doing this that your columns were syndicated and carried by more than four hundred newspapers around the country. Ann Richards shared Molly's ability to comment incisively on matters of vital importance, and to do it in a way that left true believers on both sides of the aisle in stitches.

One element of the Texas Woman brand that Molly resisted mightily, though, was makeup. She balked at both the *New York Time*'s prisspot insistence that she wear shoes and at CBS's attempts to make her over into a standard-issue sprayed, glossed, and lacquered talking head. Molly had too much Texas Woman in her to ever be anybody's standard issue. This was never more gloriously true than when she faced down cancer. Not only did Molly pass on the paint pots but, once she lost her luscious locks to chemotherapy, she even nixed wigs, turbans, and head coverings of any kind other than sun hats. Instead, she stood before us as she always had: gloriously, unashamedly, unapologetically, completely bald. Completely Molly. Completely Texas Woman at her finest.

*A*nd now, after having delivered this exhaustive dissection of the Yellow Rose, I'd like to take it all back and state that none of it applies to some of the finest, truest Texas Women I've ever had the privilege of knowing. Many of the grandest of the dames whom I've met at *charreadas*, in the boardrooms of Fortune 500 companies, in grocery store aisles, at book-slash-white-wine clubs, in university classrooms, on ranches, and in medical clinics, restaurant kitchens, church rectories, and cheerleading clinics, sport lank locks, think a mascara wand might be something you find at Hogwarts, dance like pandas on downers, and aren't particularly friendly. Some of them, in fact, are downright grumpy.

Because, in the end, it takes a heck of a lot more than queso, Dr Pepper, and hair spray to make a real Texas Woman. The single truly essential ingredient that every real Texas Woman must possess is this: she must know that she is exactly as special as the state she comes from. And there is only one TW who pointed us all in the direction of the best kind of special.

I speak of the immortal Barbara Jordan.

I came to know Barbara Jordan in 1974. And I say "know" because she was there, in my living room, that summer when all of us Seneca residents were glued to the house's television set, stunned by the House Judiciary Committee hearings held to consider the impeachment of Richard Nixon in the wake of the Watergate scandals. As momentous as the proceedings already were, when Representative Barbara Jordan took the floor they assumed biblical proportions. I stopped noticing Seneca House's lack of air conditioning on that sweaty July day when she reminded her colleagues of the constitutional basis for impeachment and defended that document's system of checks and balances that were set in place, as she put it, to "'bridle' the Executive if he engages in excesses."

Barbara Jordan not only made the case for impeachment but also helped the whole nation understand how Nixon's crimes subverted the Founders' intentions. Never before or since has a speaker made time stand still and shivers run up my spine in the way they did when, on July 25, 1974, Barbara Jordan proclaimed, "My faith in the Constitution is whole, it is complete, it is total. I am not going to sit here and be an idle spectator to the diminution, the subversion, the destruction of the Constitution." Thirteen days later, the thirty-seventh president of the United States resigned.

This utterly unprecedented Texas Woman, born in Houston's desolate Fifth Ward in 1936 to a warehouse clerk and a Baptist minister, had, from the very beginning, the quality that unites all the great Texas Women: a voice that would not be silenced. In Barbara's case, it was a voice like that of Moses delivering the Ten Commandments. Except with slightly more bass and a smidge more moral

Boots courtesy of the Texas Book Festival, a gift that went along with their Texas Writer Award.

authority. Barbara never stopped using that Old Testament voice to speak out in defense of the Constitution and for what she believed were the twin pillars of American democracy, justice and equality. It is the unsilenceable quality of her voice that the Texas Woman recognizes and responds to. When she reads Barbara Jordan's sublime words, "What the people want is very simple. They want an America as good as its promise," the real Texas Woman hears a call to action. She hears, "What the women of *Texas* want is very simple. We want a *Texas* as good as its promise."

The real Texas Woman is annoyed that she makes only seventy-nine cents for every dollar earned by men. She is insulted that only 10 percent of all elected officials are female. (Less than half the rate for the rest of the country.) And she is highly vexed that her beloved state has the nation's twelfth worst rate of poverty for women. The real Texas Woman embraces the wisdom that, if she and the other yellow roses are going to continue beating the belles of Tennessee, and upholding the brand around the world, they have to neighbor up and get the job done together.

Such were my thoughts as I drifted through HEB the other day, lulled into the particular coma that those familiar aisles induce. I don't know why, but HEB is a place of both meditation and epiphany for me. Like the time near the end of our son's senior year in high school, when, in the frozen foods aisle, I burst out sobbing upon realizing that I would never again buy Hot Pockets. This time, though, I was overcome in the cereal section.

Momentarily paralyzed by the infinity of choices I found there, I stopped trying to recall what was on the shopping list I'd left at home and began, instead, recalling all the unforgettable Texas Women who had passed through my life. The names and faces, the memories, large and small, of Texas Women I have known and admired poured over me. I thought about the famous ones, the dynamas who so decisively conquered the world that they are known around the globe by their first names: Mary Kay, Beyoncé, Selena. I thought about women in China learning how to say "pink Cadillac" in Mandarin.

Mostly, though, I thought about my girlfriends. There were, of course, the first ones, on the playground at Holy Name—as bright and plucky, as full of mischief and adventure, as the Nancy Drew heroines of my imagination. There was the one with hazel eyes who asked me to be in the court of her *quinceañera*. There was the one who was Miss

Astrodome and sang opera to the border guards in Berlin back before the Wall fell. There was the one who showered in the sun, letting the water pelt down on the necklace of tattoos across her collarbones. There was the one who wanted heroes for her students and told me I had to write about Cathy/Cathay Williams, the only woman to ever serve with the Buffalo Soldiers. There was the one who became a Buddhist nun and changed her name to something that means She-Who-Transcended-Her-Ignorant-Racist-East-Texas family. There were the two, the rocker and the scholar, who knew they were married even though the State of Texas told them they couldn't be. There was the one, barely five feet tall, who was a barrel racer with matching hat and boots before she became a Fulbright Scholar. There was the one who swam across the Rio Grande with her mother and little brother, her shoes in a plastic bag, learned English, and graduated summa cum laude. There was the one who said to me, "You never know. The best I ever had was a nerdy accountant." There was the one who crocheted potholders and wrote newspaper stories that changed the state's mental health care system. There was the one who sang her way out of poverty after a bad husband left her and her children flat. There was the one who founded a comedy troupe in spite of being deaf and now performs around the world. There was the one who nibbled halvah and contemplated how best to serve Allah. There was the one who threw her head back when she laughed her great, large laugh and held the long brown neck of a bottle of Shiner beer like a scepter in the hand of a queen.

This was a patchwork more vivid than that formed by Count Chocula, Tony the Tiger, and Cap'n Crunch. And it had transformed me. Thanks to all the Texas Girls and Women who have graced my life, the balled fist of my military childhood had long ago unclenched.

Was it possible, I wondered, that I might have absorbed enough Lone Star Lady juju myself to be able to slip through customs as a bona fide Yellow Rose? Could Lyle Lovett's immortal words actually apply to me?

That's right, you're not from Texas
But Texas wants you anyway.

The answer is not mine to give. An honor such as admission to the pantheon of the fearless, the funny, the neighboring-up-friendly, is not one a person can bestow upon herself. So, I don't know whether I can consider myself a certified member, just that it's a club I'd like to join.

And maybe you, you Texas Women, don't even take applications. But, if you do, I'd like it noted that the years that have passed since I arrived a heartbroken hippie transplant have allowed me to understand the profound importance of a good lip liner and a fine, non-clumping mascara. And "volume." Decades after knowing the queens of the Hyde Park Beauty Salon and their magnificent up-dos, as I face my own thinning strands, I can finally fully appreciate the wisdom of Ann Richards's dictum: "The higher the hair, the closer to God."

So, hey, all y'all Lone Star Ladies, if you might could be fixing to consider me for membership, tell you what: I'm a backcombing fool these days. Cuz I'm sure enough ready to reach God. The Texas Woman way.